2

LAVENHAM, LONG MELFORD
and the Suffolk Wool Country

Photographed by John Curtis

SALMON

INTRODUCTION

The charming medieval town of Lavenham lies in the heart of the Suffolk wool country. This important settlement was granted a market charter in 1257 and exports of its famous blue broadcloth went as far afield as Russia. It is said that Russian Empress Catherine the Great loved the fabric for its unique texture and insulation properties. Lavenham was among the twenty richest towns in England during medieval times but fell into a steep decline during the 16th century when lighter and more fashionable cloth was introduced by Dutch refugees. Just five miles away in the heart of the lush Stour Valley is Long Melford, famous for having the longest village high street in the country. It too became prosperous by virtue of the woollen cloth trade and its architecture serves as a beautifully conserved reminder of this time. There are at least twelve magnificent timber-framed hall houses in the village centre, two historic mansions and a most impressive 'wool' church.

The change in fortunes of these and other 'wool' settlements may now be regarded as a blessing, for development was halted and many of the original 15th century buildings remain intact. Lavenham alone has over three hundred listed ancient buildings noted as being of architectural and historical interest.

The lush rolling hills around the Suffolk wool towns remain ideal for the rearing of sheep and the famous black-faced Suffolk is now a familiar sight all over the world.

Lavenham Church

High Street, Lavenham
The profusion of half-timbered buildings in the High Street earns Lavenham the title of 'The most complete medieval town in Britain' and the jumble of crooked timber-framed merchants' mansions interspersed with small colourful cottages is a delight.

Swan Hotel, Lavenham
The Swan, dating from 1425, was a thriving trading post with stabling for fifty horses. Known as 'The Capital Old-established Free Public and Posting House', it serviced the Lavenham Machine Coach which travelled regularly to London.

St. Peter and St. Paul Church, Lavenham

Lavenham's monumental church is one of the county's finest, having the tallest tower in Suffolk at 141 feet. Standing as a sentinel over the Suffolk 'cloth villages', it was built on the success of the wool trade and funded by wealthy benefactors including the Spring and De Vere families. St. Peter & St. Paul's was completed on the eve of the Reformation in 1530 and therefore documents the entire history of the Church of England. One of its glories lies in some extraordinarily rich carving. The quality of the chiselled interior arcade patterns gives the illusion of modernity despite being crafted over 450 years ago.

Particularly worthy is a Renaissance screen around Thomas Spring's tomb and around thirty carvings depicting a star from the De Vere coat of arms. Boars feature frequently, 'verres' being Latin for boar. Less revered is the 19th century stained glass, replacing the original which was smashed by a Puritan iconoclast.

Market Cross, Lavenham
Surrounded by handsome buildings
including the former market toll
keeper's cottage, the cross was
bequeathed to Lavenham by merchant
William Jacob in 1501. It was a popula
bear-baiting venue until Tudor times
and the site of weekly markets and
quarterly fairs until the middle part
of the 18th century.

Guildhall, Lavenha
This magnificent building, now a loca
history museum, was constructed in th
16th century by the Guild of Corpu
Christi. It is traditionally lime washed
it was only in Victorian times that blac
paint was used to pick out timbers
Originally used to regulate the wool trade
it has also acted as town hall, prison
almshouse, workhouse, wool store an
club for American servicemen in WWI

Little Hall, Lavenham

One of the oldest buildings in the town, Little Hall was built in the 1390s as a family home and workplace, but in the 18th century it was split into tenements and housed six families. It is now headquarters to the Suffolk Preservation Society which welcomes the public to 'The study with 11 doors' and to admire the art and artefacts collected from around the world by 1930s owners, the Gayer-Anderson twins.

Wool Hall, Lavenham

Built by the religious Guild of the Blessed Virgin in 1464, the Wool Hall was later used for the sale of cloth before being divided into three houses. It was almost entirely demolished in 1911 but was rescued by the Reverend Henry Taylor who ensured it was re-erected on its original site.

Nether Hall, Cavendish
Originally a farm but now part of Cavendish Manor Vineyard, Nether Hall is a fine example of a Tudor building. The spaces between the timber frame were filled with wattle and daub and traditional pigments used to colour the limewash came from bull's blood, soot, chalk and charcoal.

The Green, Cavendish
Flanked by thatched cottages, inns and St. Mary's Church, the Green is a focal point of the village. It was here in 1381 that local peasants burned the mansion of Sir John Cavendish in revenge for his involvement in the killing of Wat Tyler. In the shadow of the church tower is the much-photographed group of pink-washed almshouses known as 'Hyde Park Corner Cottages', which date from the 14th century.

Clare from the Castle

The delightful town of Clare sits on the River Stour and is overlooked by the castle with its high mound crowned by an impressive fragment of the 13th century keep. Beyond the castle are the extensive remains of Clare Priory, founded by Richard de Clare in 1248 for Augustinian friars, the first house of the order in the country.

Prosperity from cloth making in the Middle Ages has left Clare with a legacy of many fine buildings, and there was also a thriving quilt-making industry. The town had a strong Quaker influence in the 17th century.

Ancient House, Clare

Built in 1473 and now the town museum, Ancient House with its superb plaster-work displays the local craft of pargeting. The decorated plaster shows scenes from the 'four continents' of the world. When the building was completed, Australia was yet to be considered a separate continent.

Gainsborough Statue, Sudbury
Birthplace in 1727 of the master of landscape and portrait, Thomas Gainsborough, Sudbury paid tribute to the artist just before WWI with this life-sized bronze complete with palette and brush. It stands in front of 15th century St. Peter's Church, one of three medieval churches in this small market town that prospered through woollen cloth and later, the silk industry.

River Stour, Sudbury
In medieval times the river was used to transport building stone, for a horse could pull up to fifty tons by boat compared to carrying just half a ton on its back. It is now a haven for walkers and pleasure boaters, including the annual 24½ mile Sudbury to the Sea cruise. Artist John Constable featured the River Stour in many landscapes

THE BULL
Old English Inn

THE BULL
Old English Inn

Bull Inn, Long Melford
The Bull, set on the longest high street in the country, was built by a wealthy wool merchant in 1450. The original timber and plaster exterior was discovered by workmen in 1935, hidden behind brick. The Drew family were landlords for over 200 years.

The Green, Long Melford
The spacious triangular green with its brick conduit is unforgettable. A long row of dwellings, all delightfully different face Melford Hall, while the final side is closed by Trinity Hospital, an almshouse founded in 1573 for twelve men and two servants.

Holy Trinity Church, Long Melford

The soaring tower, a landmark for miles around, is a happy 1903 replacement for a brick tower, built after the original was destroyed by lightning around 1710. One of Suffolk's finest 'wool' churches, it was built in the 15th century and funded by cloth merchants, most notably the Cloptons of Kentwell Hall. The windows in the north aisle display Suffolk's greatest collection of medieval glass. On the wall of the Lady Chapel, once used as the village school, is a 19th century 'times table square'.

Melford Hall, Long Melford
One of East Anglia's most celebrated Elizabethan houses, Melford Hall was originally owned by the Abbot of St. Edmunds. It has been the home of the Hyde Parker family since 1768 and has delightful gardens with this charming pavilion.

Kentwell Hall, Long Melford
The moated mansion on the outskirts of Long Melford is set in a tranquil parkland location. It was built by the wealthy Clopton family in the 16th century and the exterior of fine Tudor brick is unchanged. It has been named 'Heritage Building of the Year'.

Monks Eleigh

The Canterbury monks referred to in the village name were once lords of the manor. This rural settlement, set on the River Brett, has an attractive cluster of houses around the village green which were used in an early railway advertising poster.

Chelsworth

Julian Tennyson, great grandson of the Poet Laureate during Queen Victoria's reign, loved this pretty village of half-timbered houses. The church has a restored medieval painting of The Doom showing death, hell, heaven and judgement.

St. James's Chapel, Lindsey
One of Lindsey's historic monuments, the chapel was a chantry to the 12th century Lindsey Castle, of which only a mound remains. It survived the Reformation, being used as a barn for nearly 400 years and was donated to English Heritage in 1930.

Bildeston
Known as 'the village that moved', Bildeston, with its substantial manor house, was originally set above the current settlement next to the church. People moved down to the river valley during the 13th century, needing water for the cloth industry.

St. Mary's Church, Kersey
The 14th century parish church provides a wonderful view of Kersey and the Brett Valley, being set high above the village which was famous for its 'Kersey cloth'. The grandest aspect of St Mary's is from the south. Inside is a fragment of a medieval screen with six splendid panels including kings, prophets and Suffolk's best image of St Edmund.

The Watersplash, Kersey
One of England's quaintest villages, Kersey's main street dips down past houses that appear to be untouched by time to a watery ford where once cloth makers soaked their material. The unique ribbed fabric, especially suitable for hosiery, was mentioned in Shakespeare's *Love's Labour's Lost*. Particularly worthy of note is River House with its massive Elizabethan door.

St. Mary's Church, Hadleigh

The size of this grand 14th century church, painted by Gainsborough in 1748, shows how prosperous the medieval wool town once was. The spire is the only wood and lead example in the county and the 1280 bell is Suffolk's oldest. It is said that the Viking King Guthrum died in Hadleigh in the 9th century and is buried here. Beyond the church is the Hadleigh Deanery Gateway, built in 1495 as the entrance to the now demolished palace of Archdeacon Pykenham.

Guildhall, Hadleigh

The medieval Guildhall, newly built in 1438, represents the centre of public life in Hadleigh. It was originally a meeting place for the five local merchant guilds, with an almshouse on the ground floor, and it has since served as a school, workhouse, gaol and corset factory.

Polstead

The pretty 'Constable country' village is known for its historic 'Polstead Black' cherries. It i
also the site of a famous Victorian murder. William Corder had an affair with a local girl an
their baby disappeared. He later killed his lover whose body was discovered in the Red Barr

Published by J. Salmon Ltd., Sevenoaks, Kent TN13 1BB. © 2008
Website: www.jsalmon.com. Telephone: 01732 452381. Email: enquiries@jsalmon.co.uk.

Design and photographs by John Curtis © John Curtis.
Photograph page 23 © Kentwell Hall.
Printed in the EU.

ISBN 978-1-84640-128-3
Title page photograph: Kersey.   Front cover photograph: Lavenham.   Back cover photograph: Long Melford.

Salmon Books
ENGLISH IMAGES SERIES
Photography by John Curtis

Titles available in this series

English Abbeys and Priories

English Gardens

English Country Towns

English Cottages

English Landscape Gardens

English Follies

English Villages

English Country Pubs

English Castles

English Cathedrals

English Country Churches

Jane Austen's England

Romantic England

Mysterious England